GIRAFFES/ LAS JIRAFAS

#34 JOHN MUIR

AUG 1 2 2004

by JoAnn Early Macken

Reading consultant: Susan Nations, M.Ed., author/literacy coach/consultant

WEEKLY ⓌⓇ READER®
EARLY LEARNING LIBRARY

Please visit our web site at: www.earlyliteracy.cc
For a free color catalog describing Weekly Reader® Early Learning Library's
list of high-quality books, call 1-877-445-5824 (USA) or 1-800-387-3178 (Canada).
Weekly Reader® Early Learning Library's fax: (414) 336-0164.

Library of Congress Cataloging-in-Publication Data available upon request from publisher.
Fax (414) 336-0157 for the attention of the Publishing Records Department.

ISBN 0-8368-4000-3 (lib. bdg.)
ISBN 0-8368-4005-4 (softcover)

This edition first published in 2004 by
Weekly Reader® Early Learning Library
330 West Olive Street, Suite 100
Milwaukee, WI 53212 USA

Copyright © 2004 by Weekly Reader® Early Learning Library

Art direction: Tammy Gruenewald
Production: Beth Meinholz
Photo research: Diane Laska-Swanke
Graphic design: Katherine A. Goedheer
Translation: Colleen Coffey and Consuelo Carrillo

Photo credits: Cover, title, pp. 5, 9, 11, 21 © James P. Rowan; p. 7 © Inga Spence/Visuals
Unlimited; pp. 13, 17 © Joe McDonald/Visuals Unlimited; p. 15 © Dennis Drenner/Visuals
Unlimited; p. 19 © Peter Gottschling/KAC Productions

Printed in China

1 2 3 4 5 6 7 8 9 07 06 05 04 03

Note to Educators and Parents

Reading is such an exciting adventure for young children! They are beginning to integrate their oral language skills with written language. To encourage children along the path to early literacy, books must be colorful, engaging, and interesting; they should invite the young reader to explore both the print and the pictures.

Animals I See at the Zoo is a new series designed to help children read about four fascinating animals. In each book, young readers will learn interesting facts about the featured animal.

Each book is specially designed to support the young reader in the reading process. The familiar topics are appealing to young children and invite them to read — and re-read — again and again. The full-color photographs and enhanced text further support the student during the reading process.

In addition to serving as wonderful picture books in schools, libraries, homes, and other places where children learn to love reading, these books are specifically intended to be read within an instructional guided reading group. This small group setting allows beginning readers to work with a fluent adult model as they make meaning from the text. After children develop fluency with the text and content, the book can be read independently. Children and adults alike will find these books supportive, engaging, and fun!

Una nota a los educadores y a los padres

¡La lectura es una emocionante aventura para los niños! En esta etapa están comenzando a integrar su manejo del lenguaje oral con el lenguaje escrito. Para fomentar la lectura desde una temprana edad, los libros deben ser vistosos, atractivos e interesantes; deben invitar al joven lector a explorar tanto el texto como las ilustraciones.

Animales que veo en el zoológico es una nueva serie pensada para ayudar a los niños a conocer cuatro animales fascinantes. En cada libro, los jóvenes lectores conocerán datos interesantes sobre ellos.

Cada libro ha sido especialmente diseñado para facilitar el proceso de lectura. La familiaridad con los temas tratados atrae la atención de los niños y los invita a leer — y releer — una y otra vez. Las fotografías a todo color y el tipo de letra facilitan aún más al estudiante el proceso de lectura.

Además de servir como fantásticos libros ilustrados en la escuela, la biblioteca, el hogar y otros lugares donde los niños aprenden a amar la lectura, estos libros han sido concebidos específicamente para ser leídos en grupos de instrucción guiada. Este contexto de grupos pequeños permite que los niños que se inician en la lectura trabajen con un adulto cuya fluidez les sirve de modelo para comprender el texto. Una vez que se han familiarizado con el texto y el contenido, los niños pueden leer los libros por su cuenta. ¡Tanto niños como adultos encontrarán que estos libros son útiles, entretenidos y divertidos!

— Susan Nations, M.Ed., author, literacy coach,
and consultant in literacy development

I like to go to the zoo.
I see giraffes at the zoo.

— — — — — — —

Me gusta ir al zoológico.
En el zoológico veo jirafas.

Giraffes are the tallest animals. A giraffe can be as tall as a two-story house!

— — — — — — —

Las jirafas son los animales más altos. ¡Una jirafa puede ser tan alta como una casa de dos pisos!

Giraffes can see far away.
They can see all around
and behind them.

— — — — — — —

Las jirafas pueden ver
lejos. Pueden mirar a su
alrededor y detrás de ellas.

Giraffes have long, thin legs. They can run fast from **danger**.

– – – – – – – –

Las jirafas tienen las patas largas y delgadas. Pueden alejarse del **peligro**.

Giraffes have long, thin necks. They can reach the tops of trees.

Las jirafas tienen el cuello largo y delgado. Pueden alcanzar las copas de los árboles.

neck/
cuello

They eat the leaves at the tops of trees. They pull off the leaves with
their long, black **tongues**.

■ ■ ■ ■ ■ ■ ■ ■

Las jirafas comen hojas de las copas de los árboles. Tiran de las hojas con la **lengua** larga y negra.

tongue/
lengua

15

Most giraffes have dark spots on light skin.

- - - - - - - -

La mayoría de las jirafas tienen manchas oscuras sobre la piel clara.

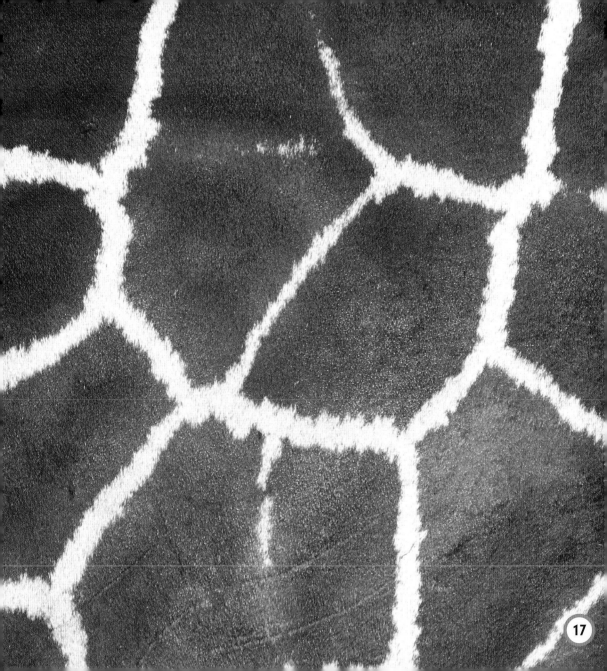

Their spots help giraffes hide from **predators** that might hunt them to eat them. Giraffes can hide in plants and shadows.

— — — — — — —

Las manchas las ayudan a esconderse de los **depredadores** que pueden cazarlas y comérselas. Las jirafas pueden esconderse entre las plantas y las sombras.

I like to see giraffes
at the zoo. Do you?

— — — — — — —

Me gusta ver las jirafas
en el zoológico. ¿Y a ti?

Glossary/Glosario

danger — something that may cause harm

peligro — algo que puede causar daño

predator — an animal that hunts other animals for food

depredador — un animal que caza a otros animales para comérselos

tongue — the part of the mouth used to help chew and swallow

lengua — la parte de la boca que ayuda a comer y tragar

For More Information/Más información

Books/Libros

Burnie, David. *Mammals. Eyewitness Explorers* (series). New York: Dorling Kindersley, 1998.

Lepthien, Emilie U. *Giraffes. True Book* (series). New York: Children's Press 1996.

Sayre, April Pulley. *Splish! Splash! Animal Baths.* Brookfield, CT: The Millbrook Press, 2000.

Shahan, Sherry. *Feeding Time at the Zoo.* New York: Random House, 2000.

Web Sites/Páginas Web

Canadian Museum of Nature

www.nature.ca/notebooks/english/giraffe.htm

For a giraffe illustration and facts

Chaffee Zoo

www.chaffeezoo.org/zoo/animals/giraffe.html

For a giraffe photo and facts

Index/Índice

About the Author/Información sobre la autora

JoAnn Early Macken is the author of children's poetry, two rhyming picture books, *Cats on Judy* and *Sing-Along Song* and various other nonfiction series. She teaches children to write poetry and received the Barbara Juster Esbensen 2000 Poetry Teaching Award. JoAnn is a graduate of the MFA in Writing for Children Program at Vermont College. She lives in Wisconsin with her husband and their two sons.

JoAnn Early Macken es autora de poesía para niños. Ha escrito dos libros de rimas con ilustraciones, *Cats on Judy* y *Sing-Along Song* y otras series de libros educativos para niños. Ella enseña a los niños a escribir poesía y ha ganado el Premio Barbara Juster Esbensen en el año 2000. JoAnn se graduó con el título de "MFA" en el programa de escritura infantil de Vermont College. Vive en Wisconsin con su esposo y sus dos hijos.